La Otra Chika/ The Other Girl

A Collection

By Vanessa Espino

Copyright © 2025 Vanessa Espino.

All rights reserved. No part of this publication may be reproduced, distributed, or transmitted in any form or by any means, including photocopying, recording, or other electronic or mechanical methods, without the prior written permission of the publisher, except in the case of brief quotations embodied in critical reviews and certain other noncommercial uses permitted by copyright law. For permission requests, write to the publisher, addressed "Attention: Permissions Coordinator," at the address below.

ISBN:979-8-218-60849-1

Library of Congress Control Number: TXu002478693

Any references to historical events, real people, or real places are used fictitiously. Names, characters, and places are products of the author's imagination.

Front cover image by Tosha Starr.
Cover Design by Andrew Espino.

First printing edition 2025.

For all my ancestors, friends and loved ones that have gone before me.

Table of Contents

MATRIARCA/ MATRIARCH
15

Matriarch	16
La Oración	19
The things I didn't see…	21
Tamale Factory	22
Citadel	27
1958	29

SOÑADORA/ DREAMER
33

Dreamer	34
Baby steps	37
Just an inch.	39
One Day	43
Soulmate	45
Dopamineland	47

BANDITA/ BANDIT
51

Bandita	52

All things are true…	55
Course Correction	57
The Secrets of Life.	60
Checks & Balances	63
OOTD: My Pink Pussy Hat	66

ROMANTICA/ ROMANTIC

73

Romantica	74
Árbol de Elección	77
The Edge	79
My Own Mantra	81
The Ruins	84
Sunday Kind of Love	86

CHIKA/GIRL

93

La Otra Chika/ The Other Girl	94
Kintsugi	100
Thoughts from Gate 404	103
Stasis 228	107
Ache	109
The Curvature of Pain	110
Untitled	113

The Disconnect	116
Wandering Eyes	118
Swell	120
4.10.23	123
Recuerdo	127

Credits

131

Artist Biography	132
About the Author	133

Acknowledgements

I would like to take a moment to give my many thanks to the people and voices that have helped over many years to bring this project into focus. Firstly Paul Collins, Angelica Lagos, Elizabeth Ramos, Avi Roque, Selena Perez, Gabriella Rincon and Willie Fortes, without whom the original spirit of *La Otra Chika/ The Other Girl* could not have been realized.

Secondly to my "Open Mic Familia", for giving me the courage to put my voice out into the world in more ways than one. For getting me in front of the mic to share stories once again and giving life to the literary community that our small town needed. To the members of House of Letters for encouraging and challenging me to keep going, keep writing just to stay in the conversation.

Lastly to my family for their unwavering support of all my creative endeavors big and small, and allowing me the space to follow those paths to wherever they may go. To Lady and Chik for pushing me to get up even when I didn't know how much I needed to stand.

Gracias a todos/ Thank you all.

Foreward

I have had the pleasure of recognizing many of these poems. Not just because I have spoken to the author personally, but because they cause me to envision a familiar axis. To be *Una Del Otras* is not to be confused with being cast out; but to recognize that each pair of eyes claims their own vantage point as the center.

In truth, there is more than one vantage point. If we look deeper, we will recognize several refractory, contradictory and complimentary personas that we collect over that grander piece of fiction we choose to call memory. Sometimes it is beautiful. Sometimes it is heartbreaking. We do not claim refraction as brokenness but as separate shades that we occasionally collate into one person, when the world asks us of it.

These poems speak to me because it chronicles those shades in exquisite detail. Lines jump from one image to the next. The layered nature of some of these pieces will ask you to sit with multiple junctions at once. They are grouped together with true-to-life details that ground you in the reality the author drags you into. What you are going to read is the result of what happens when an artist chooses to break through the block; by whatever inventiveness or ingenuity they already had, but were now, of all times, ready to summon.

Above all what you will find is the unwillingness to capitulate. There is no
need to hand over the keys to whatever treasure you have presupposed. There is no need to translate. This book is an invitation to be at the behest at what has been made manifest by the mind's eye. Perhaps a piece from another book that the author references in the next pages will provide more insight:

"That's nice. That's very good, she said in her tired voice. You remember to keep writing, Esperanza. You must keep writing. It will keep you free, and I said yes, but at that time I didn't know what she meant..."

— Adrian Hussain
Author of *Crossing the Maze*

Preface

La Otra Chika/The Other Girl has been a project that has come about in a very circular way. Originally it was written as an adaptation project, to take an artists work and bring it to the student stage at Cal State University Fullerton in 2011. My collaborator Paul Collins approached me with an artist in mind, Sandra Cisneros and her work *Loose Women*. Unbeknownst to him Sandra Cisneros was instrumental in my journey as a writer. Reading her book *The House on Mango Stree*t was the first time I had ever seen myself reflected in the binding of a book. It was Sandra Cisneros that gave me the permission to see myself as a creative writer, that my perspective, my stories and voice have a place in the world. In the spirit of the female voices she imbued in her collection *Loose Women*, the ten minute play *La Otra Chika/ The Other Girl* was born.

Now over 13 years later, I turned to *La Otra Chika* as a way out of a long period of being dormant as a writer. Life and family and loss had taken the ink out of my pen. I did not know how to pick it up, how to weld again. It took one conversation, one invite, one step up to the microphone, all those tiny steps that have culminated in the pages you have been kind enough to pick up to read. *La Otra Chika* is an examination on the complexity of being a woman, in that all of these voices the Matriarch, the Dreamer, Bandita, Romantica and Chika are all reflections of the generations of women that I have known, that I come from. Intrinsically I am them, and they are me. You cannot separate one voice fully into it's own box or category because without one the next has no foundation to spring from. Every image chosen for the mandala that covers this book is rooted in my experience, in my family, in the voices that I am lucky enough to give life to in these pages. The triumph, heartache and love that has been shared with me, that I have lived myself.

I can only hope that this collection of poetry will open eyes, open hearts and be the voice that Cisneros' was for me. Closing this loop over a decade in the making come with me on this journey in what it means to be "Otra/ Other" one page at a time.

"Women, they have minds, and they have souls, as well as just hearts. And they've got ambition, and they've got talent, as well as just beauty. I'm so sick of people saying that love is all a woman is fit for."

— Louisa May Alcott, Little Women

"*Enamórate de ti, de la vida y luego de quien tú quieras*"
"Fall in love with yourself, with life and afterwards with whoever you want."

— Frida Kahlo

"I'm a witch woman--high on tobacco and holy water. I'm a woman delighted with her disasters. They give me something to do. A profession of sorts...I have the magic of words. The power to charm and kill at will."

— Sandra Cisneros

MATRIARCA/ MATRIARCH

Matriarch

I cannot turn a blind eye any longer-
The more I see the less I am.
My people scattered, blown away at the whim of the north wind.

We were born of the earth,
The mother of all things
Children of the mighty gods
Set in the valley of the sun.

My people, a warrior people
Who responded to the Thunder's call.
Giving the holy sacrifice to the jungle spirits
Plentiful rubies of the innocent scattered before the moon.
A red river offered up so her alabaster orb would rise again,
Giving and receiving of our Mother
Until the wind changed.

The trickster north wind
Began to whisper to my people.
With promises of luxury
Promises of strength
Of splendor
Beyond what any could fathom.

The north wind sighed,
Whistled through the leaves.
Seducing one, then grabbing many
I turned away from the wind
Followed the will of the gods
Made the sacrifices to the Moon and prayed to the sun.

Our valley shook and shuddered
As the whirlwind blew around my people,
Turning day into night,
Brave warriors into frightened children
As the will of my people began to crack.

The North wind grew stronger
The whisper turned into a roar so strong I could not stand.
Taking my people further and further from our valley
Further than any had gone before
Al otro lado.

I watched our fertile valley turned sour,
Our mother's fruit spoiled and bitter
The wild rivers reduced to tear drops.
The protection of the jungle gods vanish
As fast as the Trickster North wind
Blew the last leaves from the trees.
It sucked the last breath of my mighty people
Leaving a trail of scavenged bones in its wake.

I am the mother of my people.
A daughter of the gods

I am the regal remnant,
A princess of the lost tribe.

The last protector of my people
A warrior people,
A proud people.

I stand as the last sentinel
Holding steadfast to the ways of the lost tribe
We were born of the earth, the mother of all things
We are children of the mighty gods

And so are you.

La Oración

You are there
Just on my shoulder
Plaited hair robed in rebozo
Flat encouraging stare

En tu tiempo
Una toxica
Wounded little doe
Pero exotica
Para los del otro lado

Magdalena Carmen Frida Kahlo y Calderon
Cut of your name
Slash the flesh
Broken Column
Exposed corazón

Mestiza at your core
The ribbon around the explosion
Relinquished only by bedsore
And biology corrosion

Canvas curandera
Cultura revolucionaria
Root Recuerdo

Flower of Hope
Orientar de me alma

Dos Frida's
The artist and communist
Wife and lover
Bold y tradicional
Maestra y enseñó
La fea mas bello
Palomita atrapada en chaparral

La Llorona, La Vigren y Mickey Mouse
Contained in your blue house.

Mi artista santo
Capturado en Retablo
Bless me in tranquility with
What the Water Gave Me
Guide my pen to lay bare
As My Dress Hangs There
Orgullo por me Mexicanidad
Luz en mi soledad
Still Life
El Sueño
Mi Nacimiento

Viva La Vida
Para siempre.

The things I didn't see…

I didn't see my bed today or the light come through my window…
I didn't see the first light of day or the creeping of the shadow.

I didn't see my future come until it came too late…
I didn't see the world shift slightly to push me towards that gate.

The things I saw were not expected
Now cemented in my memory.

The door
The priest
The son, the daughter
The girl and boy scared for what is to come.

I saw my rock age 100 years in just three hours…
The strength and hardness falter.

I saw the shadows creep closer the future straight ahead-
I saw my family cry and shudder.

The guiding light our matriarch going where we can't follow
The things I saw and didn't see…
The coming of tomorrow.

Tamale Factory

"You'll never know everything about anything, especially something you love."

- Julia Child

In my large Mexican family there is one tradition we hold dear, more than any other tradition we uphold. It's full of mystery and anticipation, but always heralds in the holiday season. The day that the family Tamale Factory opens is the best day of the year.

For over three generations on a single day, decided upon by the head of the family or the "Tamale Guru" we open the Tamale Factory. The Tamale Guru waits for the air to chill and the sun to mark its winter solstice before choosing the exact date to make the yearly bounty of tamales. There is a science in tamale timing that only the Guru can decipher; choose a day too early and you risk the tamales spoiling or disappearing into tempted tummies before Christmas morning. Choose a day too late and they may not be ready in time or you may not have the hands needed to help make them. Yet once the day is decided upon the Tamale Guru calls the family to gather around the kitchen table. The little four-post table in my grandparents' home is our cornerstone, the center of our nuclear universe. It is where countless bowls of cereal were slurped, pages of homework avoided, birthday candles blown out and many heartfelt talks were had.

The family gathers together, and we present the ingredients to the Tamale Guru an offering to the Tamale gods for full pots and a year without burnt orejas. Each ingredient is a blessing: Meat for the filling – to give you strength, Chilies and spices for the sauce – to bring you a year of excitement and adventure, Masa made of corn to hold the tamale together - just as the family supports you with love, and dried Orejas or corn husks to wrap the tamale in – to remind you that we all come from the earth and may return to the earth one day, in one form or another.

Once the ingredients are received it is declared, "Those that do not help cook, do not get to eat." Family legend states that, for those that do not help, the tamale may be the only gift you get to open on Christmas day. Finally it's the moment we wait all year for, the table sits hushed and it is time for the Tamale Guru to hand down the Tamale Factory duties.

It may seem silly to those who have never participated in a family Tamale factory, but for us veterans we know that the job you receive is also a symbol of the role you have in the family - in the year to come. It's a sort of Tamale hierarchy if you will, some roles are inherited others are earned but each is a badge of honor. Having a job in the tamale factory means you are no longer a child, you are part of the mechanism that keeps the family going both metaphorically and literally as we sit and prepare the family meal for Christmas morning. A job at the table means you get to hear the family stories and legends, that usually get more bawdy and scandalous as the day goes on and the wine starts to flow.

The Tamale Hierarchy is as follows: the head of the familia is always the "Tamale Guru". This is role is inherited; the title is passed down as is the tamale recipe. Only one or two people in my whole family know the complete tamale recipe and they are the ones who will one day declare the tamale factory open when it is their turn.

"The Maker of the Meat", is the next most important job, they work with the Guru in learning the recipe like an apprentice. The "Maker" learn the secret of the chilies, a much disputed secret, because only the "Maker" and the Guru know exactly how many and what kind of chilies go into the sauce.

The third job is "The Scooper or Filler," they hold the power of time. As the Tamales are assembled the "Scooper" can use a small spoonful of the meat and chilé filling, thus making dozens of small tamales and making the day seem to last forever, or they can use a large spoonful making the time go fast but then getting a smaller number of tamales. The "Scooper" has a dangerous job. Too many tamales and we are pulling them out of the freezer way past Epiphany, not enough tamales and people get angry, this is a once a year meal and if there are no seconds…well I wouldn't want to be the one to find out what happens next.

Next in the chain of command are the "Masa spreaders" this is the worker bee job of the factory. Some spend their whole lives as "Spreaders" partly because it is the job with the least risk as far as hungry Mexicans are concerned and partly because it really is an art. The "Spreaders" take the sticky, cold, raw masa on the back of the giant spoons they wield and in a few fluid movements spread the dough on the rehydrated corn husk like a master cake decorator. Moving from one husk to the next, often with freezing fingers and masa on their arms and laps, the "Spreaders" carry on conversation or family gossip and are the engine keeping the tamale factory going.

And finally there are the "Oreja soakers". The job of the "Oreja Soaker" is mainly to rehydrate the dried corn husks and pat them down so they aren't dripping for the "Spreaders" to use. They are also the catch all because once we start assembling tamales we are not able to leave until the last tamale is in the pot. The Oreja soakers pick up the trash, refill the drinks and help clean the dishes. It is a humble job but needed.

With everyone in his or her designated job the assembly line begins. Orejas are prepared for the "Spreaders", the masa is spread on the leaves for the "Scooper" to fill with filling, the "Maker" rolls and wraps the tamales and the Guru places each tamale in neat little rows in a large blue speckled pot to be placed on the stove for steaming. Over and over again we assemble the tamales until we fill all the leaves creating pots of golden tamales in our little tamale factory.

It's a long day of hard work. We stay for hours cleaning up our little kitchen table and telling stories as the tamales cook. We joke about that one time my aunt climbed out her bedroom window when she was a teen trying to go out for a night with friends. We reminisce about my grandfather and grandmother who have now passed on but had the kind of wanderlust that would urge them to throw all five of their daughters into their family van and camp on the beach just because they needed to see the ocean. All while the pots are on the stove their lids occasionally rattling as the steam spills out of them releasing that familiar holiday tamale smell.

Finally the Guru decides it is time, and goes to check the first pot. If our offerings to the Tamale gods were in our favor the Guru can open the lid. Everyone is silent again as the Guru listens for the gurgling of boiling water under the tamales to turn into a slithering hiss of steam. "They are done" the Guru declares as the first fully cooked tamale is served on a humble paper plate and set in the center of the table.

The Guru offers each of us a taste under the belief we are second opinion to check doneness. But in truth it is the final offering to the tamale gods. To all of our ancestors and loved ones that have gone on to that next place before us, as a thank you, as a way to keep the traditions that they have passed down to us going from one holiday season to the next.

 Happy Holidays y Feliz Año Nuevo from mi familia to yours.

Citadel

The strong one
The rock
The pep talk deliverer
Prospective insight seer
Tear wiper
Wisdom giver

Watching aloft, making sense of the chaos
Empath receptacle fortress.

The shielded place, the person
People tell their secrets to
For safe keeping
For transmitting
For relinquishing
Yet no one dares care for the giver of truth.

For they are the stronghold
The glue that holds the fabric
The wise one does not get to be held

And when a crack shows,
Is quick to dismiss
That all that's been bestowed on them
Is weightless.

Standing silent on precarious shoal
Takes its heavy endless toll

A constant berating
Besieged parapet
Bombardment of feeling
Erode the foundation
With waves of spent tears
From everyone else

It becomes harder to rebuild
Each time the hand is let go
To face the day

As the wise one
Welcomes a new soul
To their safe harbor.

1958

Eyes closed to the warmth of the mid day sun
Wrapped in the security of the arms that held you
Head nestled on his shoulders
Lo sabías entonces?

Serene love, quiet captured in Kodachrome
Against a white sky,
Grey water and the scratches of time
Handwritten time stamp in the corner
Like you knew
Lo sabías entonces?

Sabías entonces
That in the irises of your chocolate brown eyes
Held the comfort of three generations?
I see it.
Echoed in their gaze
Though most have never seen the shine
Your luminous smile
Reflected back a them.

Were you dreaming
Of the life written out for you
Yet to be lived.

Were you hoping for the sons
You had yet to meet
A future planned out
Before you?

Before you were given the chance
To find a voice of your own.

Lo sabías entonces?

Did you ever dream of a path all your own?
No expectations
No rules
No certainty
Just you?

All those days at the stove
Cooking to fill empty plates
Hours sweeping the mop across the tile floor
Keeping the house clean and tidy

Minutes spent in front of the mirror
Getting your hair to curl
Your cheeks to rose
Your lips to ruby
Enveloped in lily perfume

Was it for him
Or you?

Lo sabías entonces
How fleeting our time was meant to be?
The questions left unanswered
The moments I wish I could take back
Or commit to cemented memory

Did you know?

Do you know,
Those chocolate eyes
That continue to grow
Add branches to the tree you planted
Have never heard your laugh.
Never held your hand.
Will never know you
The way I did.
Will only meet you where you rest.

Eyes closed to the warmth of the mid day sun
In my quiet moments
I can almost feel you
Siento que lo sabes.

SOÑADORA/ DREAMER

Dreamer

We all dream.
Wonder what's on the other side.
Dreaming is the easy part;
It takes courage to act on them.

When I was young I had a dream. Maybe it was a vision - I was never quite sure. I was standing in the wilderness at the sandy the edge of a river. The sand was warm, enveloping my tired feet begging me to sink deeper into the soil. The dark green river flowed wide and lazily in front of me. Moonlit reflections of ripples lapping at the shore stopped only by the chaparral rooted at its bank. Across the meandering water I could see the glimmering lights of a city. Twinkling in the distance like a silver oasis of bustling life in the expanse of nothingness that surrounds me.

 I knew…I belonged there.

In the pueblo where I am from, old movies were brought to our small church every other month. My favorite was a story about a girl with trenzas y red shoes. She went into color on a huge adventure but at the end went back into black and white.

I would have stayed in the color.

Followed that golden road as far as it could go and never look back. That afternoon on our small walk home, I told my Tia "I am going to make the journey across the boarder one day."

She looked at me with her kind eyes that held a glint of weariness and said, "Women don't make that journey, la vida en sus ojos se desvanece." - *The light in their eyes vanishes.*

At 17 without telling anyone, I left my home in the middle of the night. I walked in the moonless night to the next town over where a well-known coyote lived. I woke him up by knocking on the window of his battered and rusted blue pick-up. Toothpick nestled between his teeth, hat tipped down over his eyes, dust lined boots on the dash he looked me up and down and the whine of a low whistle left his lips. He took what little money I had saved and threw me in the back of his truck.

As the sun rose, he drove out into the desert far past any roads into the dusty wilderness. I was finally going down my own yellow road heading into a world of color. I closed my eyes and as the wind swept through my dark curly hair dancing in the wake of the engine. I raised my face to the clear blue sky full of possibility as the warmth of the sun kissed my cheeks.

The coyote stopped the truck and I opened my eyes hoping to see the cool river I had seen in my vision, but there was just a small tree and more desert. He grabbed me out of the back and threw me to the ground under the wilting shade of that tree. I heard the click of his belt buckle.

As the metal hit the toe of his boot, I knew he would take me no closer to the river or glimmering city I had seen in my vision.

The coyote devoured me under that tree, ripping me apart with his hot breath his fingers digging into me like sharp teeth; as I watched the harsh sunlight dance through the leaves above me.

He took all that he wanted then drove away. Leaving me to the mercy of the hot desert with only an old milk jug half filled with water. Abandoning me, exposed for any other vultures to pick at.

It took me three tries to get over.

I followed my harsh yellow road into a city of light and I will do anything to keep from going back.

Don't hold yourself back,
Have the courage to follow your dreams.

Baby steps

Moving forward
Moving slowly forward.
Daydreaming about possibilities
Daydreaming at all-
Lighter everyday

Yet in the quiet of my own thoughts
I grow still.

Then I breathe.

Slowly in…
Slowly out…

And I keep moving forward.

Moving,
Moving forward.
Slowly forward.

Shedding the weighted blankets
That once felt secure

For something unknown.
Something wild
Dreaming of hope
Dreaming of serenity
Of Joy

As I move.

As I move forward,
Moving slowly forward.
Away from pain.

Towards you.

Just an inch.

You let me in for a moment.

For a breath, I saw you.
Unadulterated
Unedited
Not a filtered version
Projected image preened for all to see
It was you.

For a breath
I saw the boy that you were.
The child
The innocent left alone
Disregarded
Hurt
And neglected.

Reaching out for a hand
To be held.
In a blink,
Now guarded and stoic
He was gone.

I wish I had known
That I had been warned.

I would have scooped up each word
Committed to the depths of my memory.
Recalled the sound of each syllable
As it left your lips.
Held the cadence of your tale
Like your heartbeat.
Resonate and safe
In the corner of my soul

That belongs to you.

I could have frozen time
To gaze upon the golden hue
Of your hazel eyes.
Warmth and honey light hidden from view
To the world.

Let me stretch the seconds
Allow me a glint behind your guise
Expose your latent gaze
Full of hope.
Full of hurt.
Trepidation,

That how I react
May change the way I see you.
Here and now.

For a moment I saw you
When I was least expecting it
You were there
And just as fast
You dissipated
The smoke screen in tact.

Staying out of focus
Comforted by the shadows
You know so well.
The wall of humor,
Illicit sentiment
Charming innuendo
Firmly in tact.
A self proclaimed scumbag
Ready to use
And be used.
Hiding the innocent child of circumstance
You were.

You are.

I'll wait.

I'll be here
Ready to capture you,
Ready to receive all that you have to give.
Ready.

Waiting
Anticipating
I am patient
For the next moment.

When you let me in

Another inch.

One Day

One day you will be here.
One day I will feel your fingers in mine,
Your gaze locked with
A quiet knowing smile
Focused on me.

One day can't come soon enough.

One day I will feel your presence
Before you reach out to hold me.
One day this distance will make sense
The longing of endless nights alone
Outstretched in the dark
Will be worth
Waiting.
Measured in minutes, in miles.

You will be here
All those someday's
Will become real
One day.

One day together in the same time
In the same bed
In the same breath

One day.

In the snow or the sand
Doing something fantastic or simple and bland.

That "One day" keeps me going
That one day knowing this can be palpable
Solid
True

I am impatient for that day
One day intertwined,
Grounded on the same ground

One day.

Soulmate

Soul flame
Can leave you, find you.
Pick up conversation
Transposed from one year to the next
Understanding like no time has passed

Soul love admiration
A short hand, a bond
that goes beyond

They see you as you are
Know you at the core
Witness at the beginning
Will meet you at the next fork
Pushing you to keep going.

Be the best most authentic
True self touting
They have seen in you the whole time

Soul love
Emanates from a tight hug
A slanted gaze
A crack at embarrassment shared in youth
Hand held in silent consolation

At your most open and raw
Enveloped in unjudged celebration

It's always been there
This bond that can not break
Through distance
Or time
Or heartache.

Romantic love burns bright
Soul flames glow red

Like charcoaled ember
Cozy and warm
Sparked in laughter
Stoked with pride
A blazing safe haven
A beacon on a dark night

May not have known at the start
You were the missing pieces
Chosen family
Left atrium to my beating heart

Soul friend
Soul love
Soul good.

Dopamineland

Dive into bliss as you sail in a bespoken bubble
To a place where there is no trouble
Leave chaos enthralled where it lies
Come to this place of pink and blue skies
Become a new world escapee.

Taste Caviar wishes
Sip champagne, as dreams become reality.

No need to fight or quarrel
Care not for fears of mere mortal
In this land of everlasting joy
Where milk & honey flow near fields of organic Bok Choy

The sun shines bright
In this place sans plight
At a constant 71 degrees in wafting lavender light breeze.

Lux Lucite on every gleaming surface
Cleansed karma your free gift with purchase
Free of bacteria, germ or airborne particle
Sanctioned
Sparkling
Stylized

Sanitized

The minimal life here is quite remarkable

No residue will you leave in your purified alabaster habitation
With complimentary constant robotic decontamination
Only the finest apricot, almond and brown sugar exfoliation
Removes all trace
Of that dirty dead place
As you feel the purest glow, untouched soft skin sensation
If you so choose this permanent lifelong cessation

No fears of violence or death
Every day here is prefect til your last breath.
Mood stabilized and even keel
No room to reason, question, scrutinize or feel

With new viral trends uploaded on the hour
Just copy and paste, forget your need for brain power
Follow
Then like
Hit that sub for a chance at the mic
A constant outpour of validation
When you come to this utopian nation.

The cost you ask, its just the right price
Give us all that you have plus tax times thrice

For this land carefree full of excess and love

Is just for the privileged that live a line above.
Where every wish is but a command and request
And every prayer answered for the elite dispossessed.

Here everyone is healthy and tanned
DNA cataloged disseminated and scanned
Only offered to the perfect few of influence so grand
We will take the lead, you are second in command

Basal cognition relinquished in debilitation
Neural network nirvana synthesized castration
Paradise is in grasp of your self conscious abdication
Give yourself over to wondrous sensory deprivation.

Its yours to experience first hand
To all that enter this happy place,
Welcome to DopamineLand

BANDITA/ BANDIT

Bandita

Strength comes from within
Strength comes from standing up
Stand up to be counted
Stand up to be noticed
Stand up and fight for what you know to be true and right.

Those who are weak sit and wait
For the world to turn around them
The courageous stand up
And turn the world.

I ran wild from the time I walked
Bare feet, threadbare clothes didn't matter
I refused to become a comadré, and get fatter.

I rode like a charrito,
Harder and faster
Away from the grasp of any beaux
Refusing to get slow.
In those days just running
Relying on cunning
Towards blank horizon
refusing to get caught.

We found purpose in Villa and his cause
Fighting for our just and right laws
That wrapped so many men
In red stained gauze.
We found our strength in numbers
We used our strength in caliber
I fell asleep with Doreto,
Was awakened by Pancho.

From then on, I refused to fall in the shadow.
Hitched up skirt
Breasts suppressed in bandeau
Bullets on my heart
Gun at my hips
Patria soaring from my lips.

I seduced the men I wanted.
Always running fast
No time to be courted
Kissing their skin,
Sweat like sweet mango
Wrapping my arms and legs around them
Tight as a lasso

Finding my strength in their ecstasy
The pure rapture of a night of brevity.
Taking what was there
Expecting nothing more

Gave me the strength to
Keep walking out that door.

Strength comes from within
Strength comes from standing up
The brave are not infallible
The brave just refuse to fail

Strength comes from knowing who you are
It comes from the core of your being
Your substance
Your guts.

The strength you seek is inside of who you are
Not from a glass
Or sweet smoke of a lipsticked cigar

Head high
Eyes bright
Naked and unfurled

Stand up and turn the world.

All things are true…

Sometimes soy Chingona
Sometimes I'm not.

Sometimes I turn on music, cumbia clean and get shit done.
Sometimes all I want to do is Netflix and chill by myself
Open a bottle of wine to drink on my own,
A Wednesday night lush without a care for the morning consequence.

Sometimes I am the boss and delegate effectively.
Sometimes I can trouble shoot three problems,
Faster than you can ask the question
And am always right.

Sometimes I check my messages once an hour
Just to see if you care to respond.
Sometimes I yell at myself for checking in the first place.

Sometimes soy Chingona-

Sometimes I spit cultura, like water flowing from my pores
Sometimes I wear the ropa,
Do the makeup,
Say the words,
Wear the hoops,
To prove to the world how Chingona I really am

Sometimes I want to play hard to get.
Sometimes I think I don't need you
Sometimes I know I don't.

Sometimes all I want is to be held.
Sometimes the touch of your fingers laced with mine
Is enough to hold me up.

Sometimes I'm so drawn to you I am compelled
To ring you,
Text you regardless of your singular response…
 "Sup"

Sometimes I'm afraid you don't want me.
That you have already taken all you cared for
Sometimes I wonder if it was all just sex,
Sometimes I don't care that it was.

Sometimes you say I love you.
Sometimes I believe it

Pero sometimes Soy Chingona
Sometimes I'm not.

Course Correction

I look in the mirror more often,
Taking time to enjoy putting on makeup
Finding the perfect shade of berry to line my lips.
Finding the beauty in my dark eyes
Veiled in black rimmed glass
Sapping selfies.

Appreciate myself
Take the ego boost as it comes, savor it.

Learning how to be confident I my own skin
Carmel and curved,
Soft and thick,
Round where I want it and also where I don't.
Medicated to function
Sensored to monitor
Masked to breathe
Torn, broken bandaged and fixed.
All the things I don't show under crafted styled clothes.

Practice self care
Give to myself in…
Empty journals waiting to be filled,
Coffee cups needing to be sipped,
Wine uncorked,

Nails done to pristine sparking shine,
Hair bright, bold and short
Glittered shoes that light up.
Stand out for no-one other than myself.

Learning how to speak up
In new and outspoken ways.

Step inside and outside myself
All at once.
Live in the contradiction
Of being humbly confident,
And sexy.

Never forget,
You are to be respected
You are to be treated like
The goddess,
Reina,
Woman that you are.
Beauty emanates from your soul,
Resides in the reflection,
But is felt in the heart of the strangers you touch
With kindness and grace.

Don't wait to be happy.
Take the space for yourself.
Take the quiet that you need

Take yourself seriously.
Be good to your mind
Body
Soul.

Remember how it feels to…
Lay in the grass and make shapes in the clouds.
Wonder and imagine as faithfully as a child.
Be the first to stand up and dance on an empty street,
Sing in the car at the top of your lungs
Live in the moments big and small.

Above all,
Give yourself up to being happy
You have the permission
Love on yourself
Like no one else can.

The Secrets of Life.
(For the one who has already lived ten lifetimes)

Life is a puzzle,
You have to try and figure out
When something fits together, it feels right
In the core of your soul it clicks.
Move onto the next piece,
And the next,
A lived portrait pointillism of experience
Until the picture comes into focus.

Wake up each day with intention.
Don't linger in your sheets,
In your slumber.
Face the day with open eyes
Inhaling the light of possibility.
Waiting for you to grasp it
From the clear morning skies.

Move.
Up or down,
Walk, run, jump, swim
Twirl, saunter and stroll.
Move to keep from atrophy,
Move to stave decay,
Movement is the alchemy

Your body's full array.

Dwell in the ability to feel-
Everything.

The searing and painful,
The harrowing heartache,
Unspeakable misery,
Bespoken to you alone.

Honor the pain, the sadness.

Live in it.

Feel the depth
A chasm of sorrow,
Let it wash over you
To its fullest breadth.

So you can receive how boundless
Your happiness can be.

Experience the extent of joy
That is there waiting to be harnessed,
waiting to bless
As long as you can feel it.
As you come upon a solid doorway
Let your curiosity open the door.

The road may be long and treacherous,
It may take you down paths
You did not know where there.
Challenge your resolve;
Challenge your strength
Challenge the way you see the world.

Walk through it anyway.

When you get to the end of your path
And look back on the tapestry of your experience,
Your lived legacy.
Of people
Of hope
Of family,
Know that the truest part of yourself
Is brightest when you use every color in the spectrum
Of what life has to offer you.

Checks & Balances

I check all the boxes,
All the boxes that don't belong.
Face to face with an insidious forced
Thought docile or bygone.
In my home, an acrid smell fills the air
A bite to the breeze
A warning that I am no longer welcome anywhere.

Filled with uncertainty
A raging well of emotional urgency.
Far away from hope of change
Steps backwards from progress from grace.
In this country that I have grown to love
Do I still have a place?

I check all the boxes
Descended from immigrants; check
College educated; check
A successful woman; check
An ally for the disabled, aged and infirm
Waving my rainbow colors
As a person of color
Check,
Check,
Check.

The progressive threat
Realized in the flesh
A woman with a voice
The nerve speak loud and overset.

I am American to me
What am I to you?

In this new chapter of the experiment we call democracy
A roaring outcry from undesirables like me
Swells louder.
We have seen the warnings echoed from the past
This unsure footing a familiar encounter
On precarious new path.
Written on digital letterhead
The country has chosen to tread.

Rhetoric listened to as fact
Fodder and commentary as truth
An actionable agenda of countless changes
A mandate for leadership in 920 pages

Striking at the heart of checks
Knocking down the balances
Beholden to ensure
That life, liberty and the pursuit of happiness
Are guaranteed to the masses

Guaranteed for all Americans
Unless you check all the boxes

Like me.

OOTD: My Pink Pussy Hat

It trends
Its't hot
You made it yourself
Wore it for a month
Thoughts and prayers
Attitude in crochet hot pink knots

I never took it off.

You chant
You walk
Make posters out of puff paint
You fundraise
You vote
Its all righteous and quaint,

Where are you now
As they legislate my taint.

An idealized future
With peace and equality,
An ironic suture
To stave the fragility.
In the name of the framers

Who never saw me as whole or with agency.

I wear my pink pussy on my head
Not my fault if it fills you with dread.

I wear my pink pussy on my head
Tribute for the mother, the patron saint
To hold you accountable without restraint,

I wear my pink pussy on my head
Everyday in full hot pink pussy splendor
'Cause the one thing I can't change is my fucking gender.

Code switch can't reach between my legs,
Take away my choice ignite the powder keg.

Curséd Childless Cat Lady,
Sinister Educated Spinster,
Venus Deathtrap Director,
Libertine Lady of the Blade,
Feral Fanged Dowager.

Independent sensual woman brimming in wickedness
Living happily despite your cognitive dissonance.

I wear my pink pussy on my head
Not my fault if it fills you with dread.

You try and corner me
With your sermon, with your minister.
Silence me
In a proposition check box from your Senator.
Want to cage me
With Supreme Court ligature,
Try to control me
With shit orders spewed by a Cheeto Dictator?

Try and come for me.

Try to cut me down.
With your fountain ink machete
I don't get cute, I stay ready.

Flip the flag "Nation's in Distress"
Convicted, exposed by storming blonde actress.
Fill the news cycle with rampant lies consumed and replete
Pointing fingers at reason and "Cultural Elite."

It's not a show
With writers and plot.

When lives are lost
By the lies that you've wrought.

When the melanin in my caramel face
Is enough to convict regardless of birthplace.

When my sisters lie bleeding in the streets,
At home in bed staining their warm cotton sheets
Turned away from miscarriage relief.

I wear my pink pussy on my head
Not my fault if it fills you with dread.

Its not a movement to stave strife
Its a commitment for my choice to life.
A life without judgement,
Where truth and happiness are incumbent
My inalienable rights protected
"The blessings of liberty to ourselves and prosperity"
Respected.

Fashion faux pas
In your sight line
Everyday to gnaw
Until common sense aligns
Written in ratified law.

Until then, I'll speak louder
I'll cry harder
I'll pick up my sister;
If you kick her aside, I'll assist her.

Thoughts and prayers
Attitude in crochet hot pink knots

You wore it for a month

                    I never took it off.

ROMANTICA/ ROMANTIC

Romantica

"Mi Corazón" is what he called me.

He stood there a complete stranger and declared I was his heart. Right there in the middle of the square in front of everyone - he said, "Mi Corazon" like it was a fact. Days past, I saw him selling fruit in town and he said it again …yelled it from across the street, "Mi Corazón, mi corazón está contigo mi amor."

He was ordinary, he wasn't tall or particularly handsome, he had big ears and a crooked smile but there was something about his warm brown eyes that startled me. He walked me home one night, took my hand in his warm work worn fingers and kissed my palm sending a jolt of electricity to the depths of my stomach. We stopped under a jacaranda with a soft breeze blowing the lavender flowers to the ground and he whispered it again in my ear, "Mi corazón está contigo mi amor."

That night I realized; it was not his eyes that startled me it was the conviction of his voice that made me pause.

He took me to the room he rented behind the butchers store. With every step I took up to his door, I felt the drumming of my heart beat grow louder and I felt my childhood fall further and further away. In his room was a bed with a threadbare blanket, one pillow, a worn book on

the table and a pink rose bud picked just for me. He led me to his humble bed and I sat as he locked
the door. I looked up into his startling eyes as he lightly touched my cheek and said, "Mi corazón está contigo mi amor."

We made love in his dingy room but with his heart, it was a palace suite in my eyes. His body heavy over mine, his mouth hot and sticky on my neck. I gave myself to him wholly opening my soul for him to leave an imprint. When he looked at me I was the only thing he saw, when he kissed me I was the only thing he ever tasted. As I fell over the edge of delirium I whispered to him, "Mi corazón es tuyo siempre."

Two days later, he left.

The evidence of our one night soon grew within me. I held out hope of his return. That one day I would look in the street and see his startling amber gaze enveloping me again. I knew one day he would arrive again for me. That the missing piece of my heart would be restored and the echo of his declaration would be revived. For months I waited. I sat by my door at sunset every night holding vigil for any sign of his return but nothing came.

The day that his son was born, I had gotten news that my heart was stolen by a man with a wife and three kids in Michoacán.

My heart broke as I screamed welcoming my child into the world. But as fast as it shattered, it was restored when I held my heart in my arms for the first time. My dark eyes reflected in his tiny face I held my son proclaiming, "Mi corazón es tuyo siempre."

The words are only as important as the feeling, the power that you give them.

Árbol de Elección

In shade at waters edge he wakes to see
The beauty of all possibility
Her grace in repose, framed in green meadow
Soft skin untainted by mornings warm glow.

A quiet inhale, he watches her breathe
A purity unmatched and unseen.
A languid caress across her warm breast
Enamored by soft flesh curved hip to chest.

Blessed temptation of her form, by curated
Cordial pious intent. Lust castrated
Inverted reflection, forced to submit
Bound to ever long lasting penance,
In trusting of gods counterfeit.

Under platant trees, the shushing of leaves
Hides the deep rooted siren call where thighs cleave,
Paradise found in her deep cool waters
His troth tested in wondrous quarters.

Between right and wrong he can only feel.
Shaded from daybreak, boughs help to conceal
The urge he has to make of her a meal.

Chaste love stems what a curious touch reveals;
That the distance between pure heaven or hell,
Lies in the choice that threatens to expel.
El felix culpa en ellla disculpa.
Should he succumb to devils claw.

As daybreak pushes through a purple sky,
Need and want outweigh rules to abide by.
Fixated on her slumber ravishing
Fall from grace in mutual awakening.

The Edge

I laid my soul bare.
Flayed my heart and stood on the precipice
Beyond the ragged rocks
Splintered and spired.

A good wind,

A solid truth
Threatens my free fall…

It's hypothetical
Metaphor and sweet nothings.
Fantasy and simile,
What if's
And endless possibilities.

I said the words.
I asked the question.
I put myself on the edge of the sheer face
Standing on ecstasy or peril.

Waiting for your next word….

I'm here
I'm vested

In you.

When I take that next step,
Will you take it with me?
If I fall,
Is it your arms outstretched to catch me?

Take a breath.

Count to three,
        and-

One…

Two…

My Own Mantra

This part,
This unsure place
Limbo post face to face.
Insecurity welling up
From familiar depths.

Had a great time
Had a great smile,
Had a great kiss
With nothing but silence to reminisce.

          Am I too much?

The mystery of 12 hours ago
In complete focus.
Kodachrome in process
Peering through the red filter
Searching for room
To fit the frame, this 35mm.

The little voice
Whispering, cooing.
Second guessing
In the quiet.
Each move made

Each joke, story told.
Was it funny?
Was it nonsense,
Was it too bold?
Bubbling surety of connection
Unrequite…

        Am I good enough?

If I don't wonder,
I can't get hurt.

If I don't expect anything,
I won't get let down.

If I never ask the question
There can be no answer.

Stay in the stasis.

The moment between
Ignorance and bliss.

The unknowing basis.

Stay suspended
Where gravity has no say.

Of this limbo place

But above all give the grace

        And take all of me

                Or none of me.

The Ruins

You ruined me.

All the unknown expectation of what could be
I saw in you.
All the possibility of what I'm waiting for,
You own.

You dared to come into my life
Show me how to be treated
How to be challenged
Worshiped
Sexed
And loved…

You darkened my door,
Ruined all my daydreams
By making them come true.

Left holding a yard stick
Benchmark that all other lovers
Fail to live up to.

Another can look like you
Wear your clothes
Say the same words,

Only you see me in that specific way.

They don't have your hands,
Your smile
The smell of a long day sewn into your beard.

They will never be

You.

You ruined me
By loving so hard
By taking my soul
And emblazoning your own.

You cracked my heart
Imprinted my being.
Only whole when you are near,
Only true in your presence.

You ruined me.
To tattered shreds
Crumbled plaster
Cracked and strewn
Tossed aside,

Across the path
For someone else to come upon.

Sunday Kind of Love

What do I want?

I want a Sunday kind of love.
The kind that lasts past Saturday night.

I want that just woke up looking all Granuda,
Bed head out of control,
Don't care what your breath smells like
I am gonna kiss you anyway.

Kind of love.

I want a can't stop smiling
When your name lights up my phone.
Looking like a loon drinking my tea,
When I think about you quietly
kind of love.

I want that Singing in the Rain
Jumping through puddles
Gene Kelly swinging from light posts
Just because you walked me to my door
To say goodnight.

That first crush

That kick you in the shins
Get your attention
Run away across the playground
Just so you can chase me kind of love.

I want a Sunday kind of love.

I want the kind of love that songs are made of.
The love that holds a steady 4/4
I want the heartstring pulling,
Etta James belting At Last
Soundtrack to my life.

I want kicking off my shoes after a long day,
Find you in the kitchen cooking
Dancing while the water boils
And the chicken burns in the pan.
Because swaying together in your arms
Is all the meal I need.

I want that meet cute
I want the Harry Met Sally,
The Bogie and Bacall,
The Ross and Rachel,
Affair to Remember.
Cross land and sea
Meet you at the top of the Empire State Building
Sleepless in Seattle

Ryan Gosling arguing in the rain
Notebook
Kind of love.

I want the morning text
The I can't walk by you without smacking your butt,
The I have to hold your hand just to touch you.
Sharing McNuggets but not my fries
Know your coffee order by heart
Kind of love.

I want the need to have you now.
We can't make it to the bed
Tease and flirt with you all day
Need to knead my fingers into your hips
Grab your hair
Breathe you in deep
Kind of love.

The love I need…

Will let me cry,
Ugly.
Dry heaving, snot running
Unintelligible body wracking
Open raw and vulnerable
Red eyed and you still say I am beautiful
While you hand me me a tissue.

Love.

The Love that stays,
When everyone and everything else leaves.

The love I want will be in focus
All your attention,
The only one you see
I want to be the center of your universe
And I am not gonna share.

I want a Sunday kind of love.
The love that lasts
The golden glow of a life lived in tandem.
Like my parents
And my grand parents before them.

I want a love thats foretold,
Written in the fabric of the time
An unchanging constellation in the universe.
Beacon burning bright
As fact.
Not chance,
Or happenstance.

The stars may cross their eyes
Unrequited hearts lost in past lives

But here and now?

I'll wait.

For a Sunday kind of love.

CHIKA/GIRL

La Otra Chika/ The Other Girl

I don't know what I am doing.
She used to make these not me.
I have not spoken to you in a while…

More than a while.

When I was young you were like holiday decoration.
Trinkets and colors, faces and candles
Of hers.
Foundation brought out for a short time
Then put away when the window disappears.

I used to watch her,
Set everything just so
I would walk away to let her do it.
It's her ritual to follow
Not mine to wallow

Maybe it is unfair to only come to you
When I am unsure
But there are too many voices,
Too much uncertainty to endure.

They want me to change my name,
Give up the one constant since birth.

"It will be more advantageous for your professional potential.
"It will be better for your worth."

My name is too *"ethnic."*
I am too different
To fit in the box laid out
A taboo to the systemic

But what's in a name

It's just
A word.
A random combination of letters strung together
That I respond to
A behavioral conditioning
Nothing more, nothing new.

Yet here I exist,
I am too ethnic …
I am the other,
I am not you.

She told me to be something more,
"Adults don't play dress up…
"Solo un soñador
"Y los sueños no poner comida en la mesa."
Dreams don't put food on the table.
You can't survive in dreams y promesa.

I am not as strong as she was
Not as set or secure,
But even now years later
I look in the mirror and all I see is her.

It's just a name
It's just a word,
A combination of letters strung together
That I respond to,
A behavioral conditioning
Nothing more, nothing new

A rose by any other name que no?
A label to force some order
To set the frame.

I hear the word but it isn't me
It must be someone else
Because it isn't me
Brown skin, obsidian eyes and hair sure,
But that's not my label
That isn't me.
Quiet and demure

I am programmed to see
What I want to see
I look in the mirror and everything is blurred
My reflection, an echo

Of myself obscured
I am her of which you speak
But I am also here alive and unique.

I am plugged in
I'm aware
Able to see the possibility of tomorrow
Able to use the technology of today
Able to dream, to wonder
To see the rainbow connection
To be the college graduate
The creative
The political
The astute and prolific

But all you see is her not me.

Yes we are bound, forever intertwined
But I don't speak how you want her to speak
I am loud and opinionated
Pushing boundaries of the dogmatic
I am passion and flame and dramatic.

I don't know the origins of the Aztecs, Toltec and Maya
The history of Chavez of Villa
The glory of La Raza, protected by La Vigren
Because I'm not her, I'm me

The older I get the more our lines blur
I can't resolve it; it won't concur
I use her to get a scholarship
Or a leg up in an interview
And put her away as the artist
Only to find her pop up again
As she guides me to a pew

White washed
Cocoanut
Latinx
Chicana
Beaner
White-xican
Wetback

I am all of these
And none of these

I am the contradiction,
The second generation
The assimilation product of a
Suburban master planned community
The exponential cultural reality
I am the "her" that you see
I am the "me" that I am

The other girl is what you see

Not who I choose to be

I choose to be who I am nothing more.
I am everything these women were
They were part of my mother
Who is part of me.

My name es mi familia;
My name is not a label
Or diversity asset
Fulfilling that faceless silhouette
That goal unmet

I may be too ethnic
And I may not know how to build this
For you
For her

I don't know how to be the other girl
But, I know how to be me.

Kintsugi

I did it this time
This one I own.
A sliver of resolve has cracked off
Rupturing another hole in the facade
Piercing straight.
Pinholes of light peek through
The flawless porcelain surface
Of her beautiful face.
Now wrinkled and chipped.

With a single word
I suck the breath from her lungs
Crestfallen and deflated
My resolve at grips with her life force.
As I stand stalwart,
She implodes.

Over time she is slower to retort
Her wit weakens just an inch
Not so much that others can register
Just enough for me to see.

I don't choose to make things harder
I fight the urge to be selfish
A low constant push of impulsivity,

Harder to keep restrained
In perfect order.

And when it shows its impish face
Calling me into the dark,
Seducing me to stand in the spotlight
Summoning me to spin the embers,
Wild on the wind
Into golden winding thread.
Long enough
Strong enough
Powerful enough
To encircle el mundo
Three times over
Huēhuecoyōtl drawing out
Great mysteries of the unseen
For me alone to harness
As I abide his every request
Isolated in egoist rapture,

She fumbles.

I'm culpable.
I did that.
I threw hubris in the path
Made her footing unsure,
Everything she says
I have already berated myself ten times over

For even entertaining the thought
To walk into unknown void.
She's in my head
She's in my heart,
What she says rings true
On loop in the recesses of my mind's eye.

I dare to choose,
She looks back at me
With a pang of disappointment.
I have fractured her again
Years of hairline cracks,
Small splintering webs of dark veins
Slide up her spinal column

One move and she could crumble.

All the spun gold I have made
Cannot mask the chasms that I have wrought.
Cannot stop the constant scarring
On her porcelain face.

Thoughts from Gate 404

Unsure on shaky footing.
Unable to find a sound befitting
Unfounded confounded mess.

Numb.

Blood rushing through
Dilated pathways
Right atrium
Right ventricle
Right away on my way
Racing the night
Last seat on the flight.

Ticking clock
Tick tock, tick tock
Left atrium
Left Ventricle
Left alone watching
A dark giant void
Dancing lights landing and leaving
Can it hold the weight I'm receiving.

Keep typing,
Keep moving

Keep busy
Keep strong
Keep doing

Tick tock
Clicking sound of the keyboard
Of the clock
I got the call and I moved,
I got home and I packed
I get there and I'm scared,

Of stopping.

Of the hole ripped
Of the void in my mothers eyes
Present and gone in the same space.
Stuck in the moment plastered on her face

Tick tock
Tick tock
All I can do is watch the seconds
Move along the face of the clock

Keep moving
Keep doing
Keep typing
Keep breathing

Deep in
Right atrium
Right ventricle
Deep out

Push in
Tick
Left atrium
Left ventricle
Push out
Tock

Unsure of the ground that awaits
Hands shake
Decisions yet to make
Breathe for him
Breathe for me
Breathe to stop the roaring din
As passengers are asked to file in.

Unknown future
Unclipped seatbelt
Unzipped bag
Full of chaos clothing
A toothbrush maybe
The room number on scrap in scrawl
I brought my doll
My ratty old rag doll

For what I have no clue
It reminded me of the smell of home
As the plane taxis across the aerodrome.

Pull it together
Close everything safe and tight
Time to take wing
Into the dark void of night
Stay grounded in the air
Keep an eye on the clock
With each second say a prayer…

Breathe in.
Breathe out.

Into the fray
Of the unfounded confounded mess
Not knowing how long I will stay
In adrenaline laden stress

Keep moving
Keep typing

Clicking the keyboard
To the sound of the clock
Keep going
Until you have to stop.

Stasis 228

I watched

Helpless
As the door closed behind them

I sat

Listless
As one by one seats were full of strangers

Time moved forward.
And not at all.

I listened

Straining
As they spoke over a roaring din

I hoped

Breathless
As sinus rhythm failed to ring true

Time stood still,
Then not at all.

I carried

Selfless

For too long and lost my way

The waiting

Compels us
To believe in a brighter tomorrow even when

Time moves forward,

Then not at all.

Ache

Give me magic
Give me fire and ire
Give me passion and anger
Not passive pleasantry.

Give me your blood and bones
Give me life of your life
Give me your heat
Warm me from within.

Step up to my rhythm
Beat with me
As we stride together
Take on this night
Entangled as one.

The Curvature of Pain

Unblinking breath escapes bare lips
Chapped from recycled sanitized filtered air
Clench life out the room in one exhale
Under the blue green fluorescent glare.

An aching wordless wail
Wracked and wretched
Fills the room
Punctuated by oscillating hiss
Of synthesized vitality
Thrown into the abyss

Strained cords
An alien call stands aurally etched
In fixed point despair unmatched.

Feeling the slope of my spine sink heavy
As the weight of the universe settles on my chest
As gravity pulls me down and bones compress

A vacant universe
Unknown and forced to traverse
Thrown into orbit by a kind confirming hand
Of the attending nurse.

Where the luminescent silent stratosphere
Meets horizon and looms beyond lights grasp.
The curvature of teeming life starts to veer
With the rise and fall of solar flare's bask

Time stretches beyond light
Ghosts of stars shine bright
Broadcast a legacy of mass turning energy
Hurling through the void inexpertly

Expanding out and inward contracting
In parallel experience
Forced to ride the parabola
Of memories reflecting, refracting

Exponential half life sorrow
Thinking it will get better tomorrow

Until I hear your whistle in the depths of a dream
And am ripped open raw again by that alien scream.

Echoing in the in the limitless space
I see your smile mirrored on my face
Sent back to the beginning
Dwell in recollection compelled to retrace
Where joy and woe interlace
In shifting hourglass sand transporting.

A new normal landscape
In each orbital turn
A new normal life takes shape
And grief left in diminishing returns.

Living linear between two points
Embark on a rapid way
Through black and white choice
Though so much of life is lived in the grey.

In this grey between life and death
Between eyes open and last breath
When everything and nothing makes sense
Lives the curvature of my pain and stands immense.

Untitled

Tell me.

Tell me
Without words,

In the languid linen
When the moon sets
In the morning twilight.

Tell me.
When you breathe
Your unfinished desire
Warm across the peaks
Full within your grasp,

Tell me.

In lazed lingering kisses
Across my neck.
Effortless magnetic pull
Waking lucid dream

Knead your need
Into the softness of my thigh
Pliable to your will

Dive in my caramel canyon
Into the depths of unfiltered craving
Within the orbit of your grasp,

Feel me.
Satiate your thirst
In my cool reservoir
Seeping along your lips
Sticky and sweet.

Show me.

Show me.
Guide my finger tips
Along the curve of your delight
Teasing the length from your core
In the heel of my hand
As the bite of your teeth sink into my flesh
Yearning growl.

Sink into my chasm
Bespoken sheath
Anchored
Raw
Chained in euphoria
Unfurled for each other
Soul bare

Keep me.

Keep me,
In promise of your mouth on mine
As you whisper my name in whiskey timbre
Vibrating me to the core.

Keep me
In uninhibited pursuit
As we sink into delirium

And watch the sun rise
Floating in our ocean of sheets.

The Disconnect

Have I hit the part where it's done?
Have we reached the end of the story?
Where the current sets the drift apart.

The disconnect sits heavy
As the butterflies have migrated away
Into a slow hum of existing.

The chest cracking tears swept off my cheek
The rupture being torn apart
Have dulled the nerve endings
And there is nothing left to feel.

Just space.

Could anything have been said differently
To stave the pain
To stop the pinning
For soothing yet to come.

Left with phantoms of touch
Of feeling.
Phantoms of things that were never there
To begin with
That never belonged to me.

Can I live without
Without speaking
Stand not knowing
Certain of this end.

Nothing lasts forever
This kismet flame
Fated to burn bright then blow out
Illuminating the sky in ephemeral spark
Fading to ash as it falls to the ground.

The end of one page
The beginning of another
As I exhale
In this period
This time to rediscover.
And move forward.

Wandering Eyes

In a different world
On a different time line
Did we make a different choice?

In a different age
Under an orange sky
Under different stars
Were you happy?

Do you love me?
Were we whole,
In that worm hole?

If the stars aligned
And we met on that different plane
Would you forget me?
Like you forget her.

Would your child have brown eyes
Instead of blue.

In this different place,
Would you desire me still
If I really belonged just to you

In this reality that we live
Am I desired
Because I am beyond your reach?

If the sun rose in the West
And the Magnetic poles changed their minds
And you can have me free and clear,
Yours to possess
Yours to touch
And taste
Yours to love
Or fuck
Would you still want
The me that I am?

Part of me wonders about that alternate life
The part of me that's afraid of what the truth is
Am I the object of your affection
Until I am yours

And your affection moves to another reality

Away from me.

Swell

It comes in sets
One after another
Earth moving force rushing to the tempo of the moon.

One eye on the shore
The other on the vast ocean
Splitting the infinity of space at the edge of the world.

Salt spray
Biting your senses
Hitting you in the face with the relentless reality of where you stand.

Beating
Berating
Persistant erosion.

One shoulder towards the sand
The other towards the sea,
Away from the hustle of the world moving faster than light,

Breathe in
Breathe out

Rush in

Rush out

Toes sinking deeper into the grains
Grounding in soft embrace
Of Earth and foam,

Filling in the cracks
Undercut of weight you hold
Threatening to drown in alluring riptide.

One eye on the shore
One eye on the sea

Overwhelming swells,

Walls of water threatening to over take
Break across your breast
Pull down into the undertow

Until you let go…

Float.

Surrender your soul
To the tempo of the moon.

Ride the crest of each swell
The next one bigger than the first

Rising and falling in time
Rising and falling in purpose

Breathe in
Breathe out

Rush in
Rush out

Discover the peak of the crescent
As it breaks pushing you forward
Landing in the spot you were meant to stand.

Soaked in brine
In the light of day
Baptized in stalinized solatium

To rise renewed
To start again
For you alone.

4.10.23

I sit.
And wonder,
All the things to be done
All the things that can be accomplished
To-do lists written
Then scratched off.
Hard pressed minutes filled to the brim
Productive, active ticking time
Laundry begging to be folded
The clutter yet cleaned
Dishes begging for wash
Floors mopped to a sanitized shine
All the things that can be accomplished in these same seconds of stillness
Of unused time,
As I sit .

This morning alone.
I sit.

I sit.

In the still,
In the quiet.

While the buzz of the world continues to thrive outside my open window.
Vitamin D charged air begging to be soaked in
Full of desire to lift my chin to the sky
Long lashes closed to the bright blue cloudless hue
Letting the solar warmth caress my caramel skin,
Filling each pore with revitalizing energy
Taunting me to get up
Take on the day
It's there
Just out of reach,
As I sit.

I sit.
As the blue jay warbles
And bees waking up to the new spring air
Singing in concert, alive to the day
Apple blossoms,
Rosemary musk
Rosebuds sway
Wafting their life in the mid morning breeze
Just out of reach. Falling into my
Tease of a screened window
Filling my senses with all that is,
All the possibility of what could be
All the promise of what I could have been
Is there,

Just out of reach

And I sit.

I sit.
A blaring chime rings out
A never ending toll
My watch reminds me,
The steps I should be taking
When I need to stand
The water I need to drink
The beats my heart should rate
The oxygen in my blood
This time piece lifeline
A constant reminder to
Be mindful
Be active
Be alive
And yet I sit.

I sit in the moments of stillness
I sit.

I sit.
With the weight of responsibility that I am ignoring,
The expectation of who I am meant to be
Unable to do for myself
Like I have always been able to do for all those around me.

I sit.

And sit,
And sit,

And breathe…
Remind myself its not forever
Its for today.

Today I sit,

So tomorrow I may rise.

Recuerdo

In 50 years
I want to be remembered.

My portrait to be placed on my family ofrenda
Next to Frida Kahlo,
Grandma Ernestine
Y Nani.
Kindred creatives who were my foundation
Footing for my first steps
My voice.

I want my name to sit along side my father's.
He had the magic gift of reading people
Enveloping and bringing them into his universe.
The life of the party,
The found friend in the supermarket checkout line
The person you turn to in time of need.
The person I aspire to be.

I want to sit in a bed of marigold
Bathed in candlelight
Between my Grandfathers Isi
One who wielded the printed word on page

With ink stained finger tips.
The grace of a golden age movie star,
Spotless shirt tucked onto his leather belt of his leisure slacks.
The other spun stories,
Fabled truth in the dust speckled air
Dancing in the summer sunlight
From his garage throne arm chair.
Eyes wild full of wonder,
Hands work worn and clever
Barefoot indio
A teacher to everyone who ever told him no.

I want to sit beside all the rooted names that came before me
Oscar
Niche,
Manuel
Juana,
Getta,
Carlos
And Matthew.
Mi Lucha siempre conmigo.

In that place of honor I will still be here
On that altar with incense and light,
The bridge from here and there
That darkened plane
Where one day we will all awake from the dream
I will exist.

Until the day when someone forgets my name.

Credits

La Otra Chika/ The Other Girl: An Adaptation Project
Written by Vanessa Espino
Concept Collaborator/ Director, Paul E. Collins
Performed Spring 2011, CSU Fullerton
Filmed by Nicolas Lamb
Youtube - The Other Girl/ La Otra Chika: An Adaptaion Project

"Tamale Factory" December 6th 2016 – 2016 Audio Advent Calendar presented by Life Lab Notes
Written By Vanessa Espino
Produced by Silvie Zamora
Performed by Abel Arias
Recorded at El Portal Theatre, North Hollywood.
Life Lab Notes Podcast - "Tamale Factory" December 6th 2016

La Otra Chika – Acrylic on canvas
Artist Tosha Star
September 2024
Digital Editing by Andrew Espino

Artist Biography

Tosha Starr - is an emerging creative who transforms pain into art. Raised in the housing projects of the South Bronx, she studied in New York's famous High School of Art & Design, where she was exposed to various art mediums. However, after becoming a teen mom, Tosha was forced to put her passion for art on the back burner. After many years of juggling severe depression, working low wage jobs, and the loss of one of her children, Tosha made the decision to work out her tears on the canvas. Tapping into her inner child, taking inspiration from nature, and exploring with vibrant colors, Tosha Starr's art tells the story of a woman on a journey, treading the path to her healing.

Her art can be viewed on Instagram @OrionsLaugh

About the Author

Vanessa Espino - has been creative writer and a theatre collaborator for over 15 years at the community, collegiate, and independent level. She received her undergraduate education at Cal State Fullerton University with an emphasis in Playwriting. She was a KCACTF Regional finalist in 2012 for her original play *Odilia*, which was remounted for the Hollywood Fringe Festival 2016. At the 2016 Hollywood Fringe Festival, *Odilia* won an inaugural Hollywood Fringe Scholarship and Inkwell Playwrights Promise awards and received a Beyond Bechdel-Wallace Award nomination. Other recent plays include: *I Live in Your World* produced by CSUF Department of Theatre & Dance with NAMI and OCHCA at Grand Central Theatre in Santa Ana Ca. in May of 2013. *Choosing Us** written in collaboration & commissioned for Evolve Theatre company and premiered at the Long Beach Playhouse, Studio Theatre in Long Beach Ca. in March of 2016.

In June of 2017 she was part of the inaugural cohort of Next at the Braid Fellowship with The Jewish Women's Theatre company out of Santa Monica California.

She has also been a contributor to Life Lab Notes Podcast in 2016 for the *Audio Advent Calendar* and 2021 in the *Crockpot Chronicles*. Most currently she is a Co-Producer of Words Bubbles an Open Mic Collaborative in Tracy Ca. and works as a Community Services Director for San Joaquin County.

www.ingramcontent.com/pod-product-compliance
Lightning Source LLC
Chambersburg PA
CBHW071119160426
43196CB00013B/2628